POPE'S COCKTAILS AT HOME

POPE'S COCKTAILS AT HOME

ISBN 13 (print): 978-1-937513-93-1
First edition

Published by Cooperative Press
http://www.cooperativepress.com

Recipes and text ©2019 Clark Pope
Photos ©2019 Jeremy Fear
Narrative editor: Matt Bailey

Every effort has been made to ensure that all the information in this book is accurate at the time of publication; however, Cooperative Press neither endorses nor guarantees the content of external links referenced in this book.

If you have questions or comments about this book, or need information about licensing, custom editions, special sales, or academic/corporate purchases, please contact Cooperative Press: info@cooperativepress.com or 10252 Berea Rd, Cleveland, Ohio 44102 USA

No part of this book may be reproduced in any form, except brief excerpts for the purpose of review, without prior written permission of the publisher. Thank you for respecting our copyright.

FOR COOPERATIVE PRESS

Senior Editor: Shannon Okey
Layout Assistant: Kim Richardson
Layout Assistant: Emily Kuhn

POPE'S COCKTAILS AT HOME

Quick Recipes for Drinks and Dinner

TABLE OF CONTENTS

Foreword — 7
Bloody Mary: a request, a journey, a brand — 8
Glassware — 10
Tools — 12

Pope's Bloody Mary Mix — 14
Pope's Blueberry Lemon Cocktail Syrup — 16
Pope's Dirty Martini blend — 17
Pope's Lavender Lemon Cocktail Syrup — 18
Pope's Mint Cocktail Syrup — 19
Pope's Orange Habanero Cocktail Syrup — 20
Pope's Orange Vanilla Cocktail Syrup — 21
Pope's Pumpkin Spice Cocktail Syrup — 22

Classic Bloody Mary — 24
Blueberry Vodka Lemonade — 26
Batched Lemonades — 28
Cleveland Does A Cosmo — 30
Jason's Dirty BloodyTini — 32
Mules: Moscow and otherwise — 34
Orange Dreamsicle — 36
Peach Refresh — 38
Peppermint Bark — 40
Pope's Glacier — 42
Pumpkin Pie Martini — 44
Spa Treatment — 46
The Basic — 48
Thyme for Blueberry — 50
Dirty Is Good — 52
Gin and Juice — 54
Gin Fling — 56
Lavender Gin-Ginger Punch — 58
Lavender Lemon Spritz — 60
Hair Cut — 62
A Midnight Storm — 64
A Pirate's Pumpkin — 66

Classic Mojito — 68
Fall Harvest — 70
Orange You Glad — 72
Pope's Island Tea — 74
Spring Fling — 76
Pope Looks at 45 — 78
Blueberry Old Fashioned — 80
Kentucky Blues — 82
Pope's Family Mint Julep — 84
The Pope of Slavic Village — 86
The Big Peach — 88
My Last Night in Tijuana — 90
Orange Vanilla Margarita — 92
Spicy Paloma — 94
Flaming River — 96
Beer + Bloody = A Good Time — 98
Dragon's Tongue — 100
Lavender Pisco Sour — 102
Southern Fall Harvest — 104
The French Resistance — 106

Bloody Grilled Shrimp Shooter — 108
Bloody Mary Chili — 110
Bloody Shrimp Diablo — 112
Butter — 114
Dirty Mediterranean Salad — 116
Pope's Paella — 118
Sodas — 120
Spanish Chicken — 122
Steak It Dirty — 124
Whipped Cream — 126

Sources and Acknowledgements — 123

FOREWORD

Why a cocktail book?

It all started at a party, so I figure, let the good times roll.

In the summer of 2009, my wife was doing cancer research and participating in the Susan G. Komen Breast Cancer 3 Day Walk. To raise money for the cause, we threw a party. The concept was simple—come over, eat some barbecue, have a good time, and make a goodwill donation to the Foundation. People have always said, "This sauce is great, Clark! You should sell it!" which is a lovely compliment.

However, one of the guests at the party, Trevor Clatterbuck, founder of Fresh Fork Market, a farm share program in Cleveland, said it differently, "Make this from local tomatoes, and I will buy it."

Challenge accepted! We found the tomatoes, and I got to work on making 250 pints for him. Using a twenty-two-quart roasting pan, I spent my summer off from teaching devoted to this fun project. Trevor sold all of the sauce over Labor Day weekend. I took the money I earned and bought myself a snow blower, thinking it was nothing more than a nice perk. Little did I know that a business had been born. In the following years, I created over a dozen products for Fresh Fork Market, which led to the creation of my Bloody Mary Mix in the Fall of 2013.

Now, Pope's Kitchen is a growing company with over 20 products for sale in Ohio—12 of which are created to bring happy hour back to the home. Solidifying the Pope's Kitchen brand as the go to for delicious cocktails, along with growing the company throughout the past decade has meant lots of learning and changes; however, I have never strayed from the belief that Pope's would always be how you would make it if you had time.

—Clark Pope

BLOODY MARY: A REQUEST, A JOURNEY, A BRAND

My first foray into the world of cocktails came in the late summer of 2013. Trevor asked me to come help him at a Fresh Fork pick up location. Having developed a reputation within the Fresh Fork community for developing tasty tomato sauces, several people recognized the brand when I introduced myself. Working as a greeter and checking in the families for pick up, one gentleman called out for a local bloody mary mix, and the group agreed that this would be a great add-on item for Thanksgiving—family, friends, and local cocktails.

As the son of a librarian, I spent roughly six weeks reading every recipe, creation story, and history of the Bloody Mary I could find. Sticking to my belief that anything I created would have to be as pure and simple as possible. I set my goal to create the perfect Bloody Mary-everything in the bottle, all the spice, citrus, and depth I could manage—I kept to my roots, literally, slicing and grinding fresh horseradish so as to avoid the chemicals used by most commercial producers.

What we serve today as Pope's Bold & Spicy Bloody Mary Mix is the fourth version of the recipe I developed, featuring fresh horseradish and jalapenos for the heat and depth, rounded out with the original Lea & Perrins Worcestershire Sauce. As you can see, Pope's Kitchen has grown and developed since those early days, and it has been quite an adventure.

GLASSWARE

While people will tell you that a certain drink must be made in a specific glass or the world stops spinning the Solo Company has proven that a big red cup is really all that you need. However, we have grown up a little, and what follows is a review of the glassware featured in this book. Feel free to use what you already have at home, or you can hit the thrift store and see what fun glassware you find.

The Pint Glass: 16 oz.

Traditionally this is what you would use for beers and Bloody Marys.

The Rocks Glass: 8-10 oz.

The standard glass will hold between 8-10 oz. This is the most-called for glass in the book.
It is often referred to as an Old Fashioned Glass, a name derived from its most famous drink.

The Collins Glass: 8-12 oz.

This is the elongated version of the rocks glass, most often used for sodas and spritzers. It is narrow and tall, limiting the surface area from which the bubbles can escape.

Martini Glass: 5-7 oz.

The most iconic of all cocktail glass shapes, the stem lifts the drink up and away from your hand, keeping the beverage cold. This glass is used for cocktails not served over ice.

Champagne Flute: 5-7 oz.

While not often used for mixed cocktails, these elegant glasses are a must for any home bar, as champagne is always in fashion.

A rule of thumb is that, whenever possible, choose the smaller glass. This will allow you to enjoy your cocktail before it gets warm, and, if warranted, there's always time for a second round.

Please note, all drinks may be consumed in whatever tin cup or chalice you have laying around.

TOOLS

Jigger

A graduated multi ounce unit that will measure .25 oz. up to 2 or 3 oz. A classic flip style that does one measurement per side.

The majority of the recipes in this book are written to make two cocktails at a time, so if you have the means to measure .5 oz. up to 3 oz. you are covered.

Bar spoon

This is a spoon with an extra-long shaft, perfect for reaching to the very bottom of a glass or pitcher. The bowl of the spoon typically measures one teaspoon.

Cocktail Shaker

These come in two styles; the three-piece Cobbler Shaker, and the two-piece Boston Shaker. The Cobbler Shaker is very simple to set up, consisting of a large tin to build your drink, the integrated strainer, and a cap. It has a built-in strainer.

The Boston Shaker is made up of two tins, or a tin and a glass. Build your drink in the larger tin and use the small tin to add ice and as the lid. Tap firmly to set the small tin as the lid, shake quickly, and then tap on the side of the large tin to release the smaller top tin. This is the shaker most often seen in a professional bar setting. It is my preference for speed, and several online videos will show you how to best use the two-piece strainer.

Cocktail Strainer

There are three different cocktail strainers: a Hawthorne, a Julep, and a fine mesh. In this book, we only make use of the Hawthorne strainer.

The Hawthorne strainer is made up of a flat piece of metal and a wire spring. It easily fits to both a shaker tin and a pint glass. To use, place strainer over the container so the spring sits along the edge and then tilt so that the liquid is strained through the spring and holds back any ice, herbs, or citrus.

Yarai Glass

Named for the diamond pattern cut into the glass, this is a mixing glass, most often used when stirring a drink. This can be replaced by a pint glass if needed.

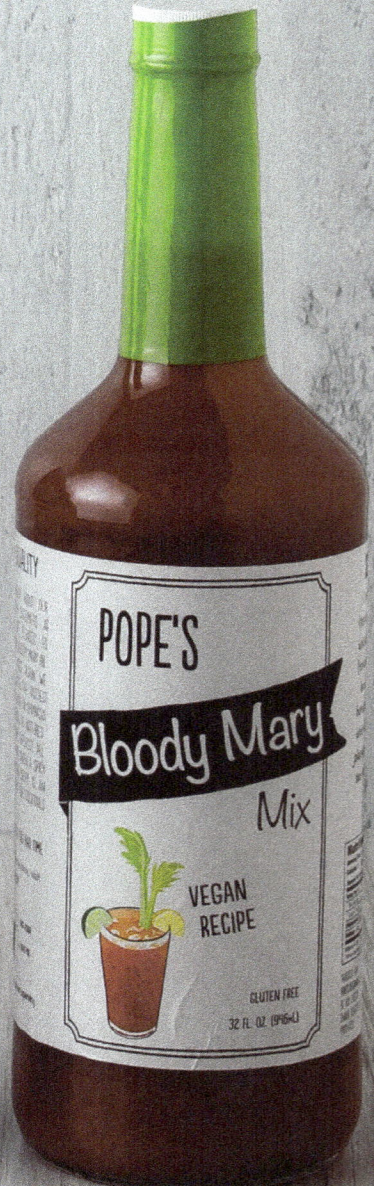

POPE'S BLOODY MARY MIX

Pope's Bloody Mary-Bold and Spicy
This award winning product started out as simply Pope's Bloody Mary, and it was meant to be the only bloody mary blending all the flavors, the spice, and the richness of the tomatoes. What more could ever be warranted? Well, it turned out that something with a little less heat was very much desired. 2014 Cleveland Magazine – Best of Cleveland, 2019 Drunken Tomato Silver Medal Winner

Pope's Bloody Mary-Traditional
My very first restaurant, Market in Rocky River, asked to carry my new creation as part of their award-winning local brunch. Market has a bloody mary cart featuring 36 different toppings, including a great selection of spices and hot sauces. On my debut, a customer over-spiced her drink, and I quickly realized that the perfect spicy bloody mary for the home would not play well at a bloody mary bar. I had to do something, so I left the restaurant mid-service and returned an hour later with the new Pope's Mellow Mary. This is now our number one selling product, labeled as Pope's Bloody Mary Traditional. 2019 Drunken Tomato Gold Medal Winner

Pope's Bloody Mary-Vegan
While sampling product in a local store, I kept getting requests for a vegan bloody mary. I pulled the Worcestershire sauce out of my Bold and Spicy recipe, creating a slightly thinner version while reducing the sodium content to only 10 mg. per 4 oz. serving. This is now the lowest sodium in a commercially available bloody mary mix.

I am proud to note that Pope's Bloody Mary Mixes are all so pure, you can find all of their ingredients at your local grocery store. And just as when I started, I still buy all of our tomatoes from along the Ohio / Indiana border.

POPE'S BLUEBERRY LEMON COCKTAIL SYRUP

During a Cleveland winter, there are always discussions of summer. In March of 2018, I sat down with my friend Courtney Koening, the Ohio Area Manager for Tito's Handmade Vodka to discuss ways to work together. Courtney has been a great and vocal supporter of the Pope's brand for many years, and the discussion soon turned to summer festivals. Tito's Handmade Vodka for years has been blended with lemonade for a quick summer refresher, so what new and fun thing could Pope's bring to the table? I don't know what exactly sparked the idea, but blueberry was quickly decided to be the next new thing for summer 2018. After that meeting, I began a deep dive to source and create the incredibly multifaceted Pope's Blueberry Lemon Cocktail Syrup offered today.

You'll find it in these recipes:

Blueberry Lemonade
Batched Lemonades
Soda
Mules
A Midnight Storm
Blueberry Old Fashioned
Kentucky Blues – Award Winning Cocktail
Peach Refresh
Thyme for Blueberry
Whipped Cream
Butter

POPE'S DIRTY MARTINI BLEND

A classic is a classic because it is always a good idea. There are so many ways to make a martini, but every dirty martini must have olive brine. And it is the quality of the brine that sets a great dirty martini apart from, well, just dirty. Always looking to improve on a good idea, I used the brine from my favorite olives, blended with a touch of fresh lemon juice, and, just like that, the best Dirty Martini Blend I have ever tasted was born. It helps that I import the brine from salt cured olives out of central Spain, but when you start with the best, you end with the best.

You'll find it in these recipes:

Dirty is Good
Jason's Bloody Martini
My Last Night in Tijuana
Dirty Mediterranean Salad
Spanish Chicken
Steak it Dirty

POPE'S LAVENDER LEMON COCKTAIL SYRUP

For some, lavender reminds them of grandma's house or the soft aroma of a spring breeze. For me, it is all about the spritz and gin. Much like many of the Pope's products, this was a result of collaboration. Partnering with Watershed Distillery from Columbus, OH on the bar service during the Cleveland Flea, it was important to be able to quickly create and serve drinks that would be appealing and refreshing. In 2010, Watershed Distillery created an award winning new American-style gin distilled with orange, lemon, lime, and grapefruit peels. My Lavender Lemon Cocktail Syrup was originally developed to match perfectly with this gin, but I have found so many creative ways to use this syrup over the years.

You'll find it in these recipes:

Lavender Gin-Ginger Punch
The French Resistance
Lavender Pisco Sour
Gin Fling
Lavender Lemon Spritz
Whipped Cream
Butter

POPE'S MINT COCKTAIL SYRUP

Due to my inability to play basketball, my family was asked to move out of Kentucky when I was seven. We moved north, bringing with us a love of college basketball, horses, and bourbon. My father started the UK Alumni Association in Northeastern Ohio, and he made sure I understood to stand at the "Call to the Post," knew all the words to my "Old Kentucky Home," and knew how to make a proper mint julep. Some of my fondest memories are of my time in bourbon country with my father, and those memories helped to forge this delightful syrup. Made with fresh mint, cane sugar, and a squeeze of fresh lemon juice, Pope's Mint Cocktail Syrup elevates anything it becomes part of.

You'll find it in these recipes:

Pope Family Mint Julep
Mojito
Lemonade
Mule
Kentucky Blues – Award Winning Cocktail
Peppermint Bark
Pope looks at 45
Peach Refresh
The Big Peach
Soda
Spring Fling
Spa Treatment

POPE'S ORANGE HABANERO COCKTAIL SYRUP

Some things just happen. I spend a lot of time in the kitchen making hot sauces, which at times means that when I get home, my hands are still burning from the capsaicin. This burn can take hours to wear off, so I will often read cookbooks and cocktail books to relax. I think this is why I awoke one morning thinking what people needed was a spicy orange syrup. Carefully crafted using fresh-squeezed orange juice and fresh habaneros, you taste first the sweetness of the cane sugar, then the tartness of the orange juice, and just when you are asking "Where is the heat?" you get a pleasant burn on the back of your tongue. Pure and simple, this syrup works well behind the bar and in the kitchen.

You'll find it in these recipes:

Flaming River – Award Winning Cocktail
My Last Night in Tijuana
Spring Fling
Dragon's Tongue
Gin and Juice – Award Winning Cocktail
Pope of Slavic Village
Spicy Paloma – Award Winning Cocktail
Cleveland Does a Cosmo
A Pirate's Pumpkin
Whipped Cream
Butter

POPE'S ORANGE VANILLA COCKTAIL SYRUP

On the same day that I was creating the Orange Habanero syrup, I was thinking, "But what about the people who don't like the heat? What fun things can I do with all this orange juice?" Then I had an epiphany. One of my most favorite summer food memories is of the classic push pop-that soft, creamy orange "ice cream" from my younger years. In pursuit of that flavor, I decided to blend whole vanilla beans into fresh-squeezed orange juice with cane sugar and a touch of water. This syrup is a deluge of vanilla and orange flavor, and when it is blended with vodka and a little ice, it is like summer clouds have wrapped you in a happy blanket.

You'll find it in these recipes:

Orange Dreamsicle
Pope's Glacier
Vanilla Margarita
Orange You Glad
Pope's Island Tea
Whipped Cream
Butter

POPE'S PUMPKIN SPICE COCKTAIL SYRUP

This is what the end of August smells like and what fall is made for. Thank you, large coffee company! Although I have never been a coffee drinker, nor have I been a big fan of pumpkins, I am even less of a supporter of large companies pushing their flavored junk on people. With some light prodding from friends, I created this syrup that is actually made using whole pumpkins. Sticking to my firm belief in providing a product that you would make at home if you had the time, I incorporated cane sugar and everyone's favorite pie spices. What I found was that I had developed a versatile syrup that would satisfy everyone's fall desires.

You'll find it in these recipes:

Pumpkin Pie Martini
The Basic
A Pirate's Pumpkin
Fall Harvest
Southern Fall Harvest
Whipped Cream
Butter

CLASSIC BLOODY MARY

Pope's Bloody Mary Mix became the unexpected flagship of the company, quickly building a following wherever it popped up. We have three versions of mix: Original Bold and Spicy, Traditional, and Vegan. Each one of these carries its own flavor profile and texture. You like it thick and spicy? Go Bold. You want to play with your drink and dress it up? The Traditional s for you. You love the spice but prefer your drink thinner? Check out the Vegan.

You Will Need:
4 oz Pope's Bloody Mary Mix
2 oz vodka
1 cup of ice

Tools & Glassware:
1 pint glass or large rocks glass
Shaker set*

Garnish:
Bacon, cheese cubes, shrimp, celery, carrot, olives, pickle

Method:
1. Measure liquids into your shaker.
2. Add ice to the shaker*.
3. Shake until a light frost forms on the tin – roughly a 10 to 15 count.
4. Pour into your glass.
5. Garnish with all the fun things.

*Don't have a shaker set? Roll the cocktail with half the ice between two pint glasses four times, garnish and serve.

Make it your own! Notes...

Alternatives
Replace the vodka with tequila
Replace the vodka with club soda
Use 1 oz of Jägermeister

Personal Tweaks

I should drink this with:

BLUEBERRY VODKA LEMONADE

I love lemonade! What's not to love about it? It's tart, refreshing, and easy to make; but that doesn't mean it has to be boring. My friend Courtney, the Ohio area manager for Tito's Handmade Vodka, shared the same thought, and requested that I make a blueberry cocktail syrup. So I did, and this riff on the classic lemonade is the best way to enjoy it.

You Will Need:

1.5 oz Pope's Blueberry Lemon
7 oz lemonade
3 oz Tito's Handmade Vodka
2 cups of ice, divided

Tools & Glassware:

2 rocks glasses
Jigger
Bar spoon

Garnish:

Half lemon wheel
Three blueberries

Method:

1. Build the beverage directly into two rocks glasses.
2. Distribute the ice evenly among glasses.
3. Add Tito's Handmade Vodka to ice.
4. Pour Pope's Blueberry Lemon Cocktail Syrup over ice.
5. Add lemonade.
6. Stir to combine using the bar spoon.
7. Garnish the glasses with lemon wheel and blueberries.

Make it your own! Notes...

Alternatives

Instead of stirring, roll ice between two glasses before pouring in liquids, or substitute watermelon juice for the lemonade.

Personal Tweaks

I should drink this with:

BATCHED LEMONADES

Preparing for a party can be stressful, but you can bring that down a notch by pre-batching your drinks. When I host a shindig, I try to have at least one quick batched beverage ready at the start of the event. Doing so frees up time and energy for any last-minute details, and pre-batching also allows you to interact your guests as they serve themselves.

You Will Need:

8.5 oz Pope's Cocktail Syrup
38 oz lemonade
17 oz Tito's Handmade Vodka

Tools & Glassware:

Half-gallon pitcher
Whisk
Large bowl of ice for serving

Garnish:

Lemon wedges

Method:

1. Measure one liquid at a time into pitcher, whisking between each addition.
2. Store pitcher in the refrigerator the night before your get-together.
3. When guests arrive, remove pitcher from fridge and whisk, as the beverage may have settled.
4. Allow guests to serve themselves and add lemon wedges for garnish.

*To offer as a non-alcoholic option, do not add the booze to the pitcher. Instead, leave a bottle and jigger next to the container so your guests can add their own.

Make it your own! Notes...

Alternatives

Replace ice cubes with frozen lemonade.
Replace the vodka with bourbon.

Personal Tweaks

I should drink this with...

CLEVELAND DOES A COSMO

Sex in the City may have ruled the nineties with its depictions of wealth and life in New York. Here in the new millennium in Cleveland, we keep things a little more grounded. A Cosmo is just a cranberry vodka punching above its weight class. Blend the cranberry and lime with a touch of spice and now you are drinking in the big leagues.

You Will Need:

1.5 oz Pope's Orange Habanero Syrup
4 oz cranberry juice
3 oz vodka
1 oz lime juice
2 cups of ice, divided

Tools & Glassware:

2 martini glasses
Hawthorne strainer
Shaker set*
Jigger

Garnish:

Half of a lime wheel
Three cranberries

Method:

1. Pre-chill the martini glasses by filling with ice while preparing the drink.
2. Add half the ice to the shaker*.
3. Pour Pope's Orange Habanero Cocktail Syrup, cranberry juice, lime juice, and vodka into the shaker.
4. Shake until a light frost forms on the tin – roughly a 10 to 15 count.
5. Discard the ice from the pre-chilling.
6. Strain beverage into each glass, a little into each glass at a time so that they both end with light foam on top.
7. Garnish the glasses with lime wheel and cranberries.

* Don't have a shaker set? Roll the cocktail with half the ice between two pint glasses four times, and then strain into the correct glassware, garnish and serve.

Make it your own! Notes...

Alternatives

Replace cranberry juice with pomegranate juice.

Personal Tweaks

I should drink this with...

JASON'S DIRTY BLOODYTINI

I met Jason, a bloody mary blogger from Chicago, when he was in Cleveland visiting family. After a delightful lunch with bloody marys, I gave him a tour of my warehouse, and sent him home with some fun things to play with. Here Jason kindly shares his creation. You can follow Jason on Instagram (@eatdrinkandbloodymary) for more reviews and updates on his bloody mary adventures. Also check out his blog for all things bloody marys (eatdrinkandbloodymary.com). Please note Jason used the original Pope's Cocktail Olives juice, and here we substitute with the Pope's Dirty Martini Blend.

You Will Need:
4 oz Pope's Bloody Mary Mix
3 oz vodka
½ oz Pope's Dirty Martini Blend
½ oz pickle juice
2 cups of ice, divided

Tools & Glassware:
2 martini glasses
Hawthorne strainer
Shaker set*
Jigger

Garnish:
Olives and pickle skewer

Method:
1. Properly chill your glassware, divide half of the ice into each glass.
2. Add remaining ice to the shaker*.
3. Add Pope's Bloody Mary Mix, Pope's Dirty Martini Blend, pickle juice, and vodka to the shaker.
4. Shake until a light frost forms on the tin—roughly a 10 to 15 count.
5. Discard the ice from pre-chilling the martini glasses.
6. Strain beverage into the martini glasses.
7. Garnish the glasses with olives and pickle skewer

Don't have a shaker set? Roll the cocktail with half the ice between two pint glasses four times, then strain, garnish and serve.

Make it your own! Notes...

Alternatives
Swap vodka for tequila or gin
Use bacon as a swizzle stick

Personal Tweaks

I should drink this with...

MULES: MOSCOW AND OTHERWISE

Like most people, I thoroughly enjoy a great story. Vodka was not a popular spirit in America during the early 20th Century, but that changed in 1947. Instant photography became a reality as a result of the Polaroid Land Camera, and John G. Martin, the American distributor of Smirnoff, used his in an ingenious marketing strategy. He would take a picture of a bartender holding a bottle of Smirnoff in one hand and a copper mug in the other, and would show it to a rival establishment. This sparked competition between local bars, and Smirnoff Vodka sales began to take off. Thus, the Moscow Mule became wildly popular. While I do think the Moscow Mule is okay, I decided to augment this well drink from the Truman years with my delicious cocktail syrup.

You Will Need:

1 oz Pope's Blueberry Lemon
3 oz vodka
7 oz ginger beer
2 cups of ice, divided

Tools & Glassware:

2 copper mugs or Rocks glasses
Bar spoon
Jigger

Garnish:

Half lime wheel

Method:

1. Build the beverage directly in copper mugs or rocks glasses.
2. Distribute ice evenly among mugs or glasses.
3. Add vodka to ice.
4. Pour Pope's Cocktail Syrup into vodka.
5. Stir to combine, then add ginger beer.
6. Stir again, gently.
7. Garnish with lime wheel.

Make it your own! Notes...

Alternatives

Swap out Pope's Blueberry Lemon with Pope's Orange Habanero or Pope's Mint Cocktail Syrup.
Swap out vodka for bourbon.

Personal Tweaks

I should drink this with...

ORANGE DREAMSICLE

Sweet dreams are made of these, who am I to disagree? This is the first cocktail I made with the Orange Vanilla Cocktail Syrup. I took it as a test product to an event I hosted, and when I ran out, it almost caused a brawl.

You Will Need:

1.5 oz Pope's Orange Vanilla Cocktail Syrup
3 oz Tito's Hand Made Vodka
4 oz club soda
2 cups of ice, divided

Tools & Glassware:

2 rocks glasses
Shaker Set*
Jigger
Hawthorne strainer

Garnish:

Orange slice

Method:

1. Divide half the ice into each glass.
2. Add remaining ice to the shaker*.
3. Add Pope's Orange Vanilla Cocktail Syrup, and vodka to the shaker.
4. Shake until a light frost forms on the tin – roughly a 10 to 15 count.
5. Add the club soda to the shaker
6. Strain beverage into the rocks glasses.
7. Garnish the glasses with orange slice.

*Don't have a shaker set? Roll the cocktail with half the ice between two pint glasses four times, then strain, garnish and serve.

Make it your own! Notes...

Alternatives

Replace the Orange Vanilla Syrup with Pope's Orange Habanero Cocktail Syrup.
Replace the rum with vodka.

Personal Tweaks

I should drink this with...

PEACH REFRESH

We keep so much peach tea from our friends at Inca Tea on hand, it's like Georgia is on my mind. So, during midsummer, when the days are long and you feel all the heat, these classic flavors make an after-dinner drink so soft you simply sink into the sunset.

You Will Need:

1 oz Pope's Blueberry Lemon Cocktail Syrup
.5 oz Pope's Mint Cocktail Syrup
3 oz vodka
6 oz Peach Tea: Inca Tea
2 cups of ice, divided

Tools & Glassware:

2 rocks glasses
Hawthorne strainer
Shaker*
Jigger

Garnish:

Blueberries
Fresh mint

Method:

1. Measure the cocktail syrup, tea, and vodka into your shaker.
2. Add half the ice to the shaker*.
3. Distribute the remaining ice evenly among two rocks glasses.
4. Shake until a light frost forms on the tin – roughly a 10 to 15 count.
5. Strain into rocks glasses, filling half into each glass then topping off.
6. Garnish the glasses with blueberries and mint.

* Don't have a shaker set? Roll the cocktail with half the ice between two pint glasses four times, and then strain into the correct glassware, garnish, and serve.

Make it your own! Notes...

Alternatives

Use frozen peaches for half the ice

Personal Tweaks

I should drink this with...

PEPPERMINT BARK

While summer may be the heart of the cocktail season, the soul of the cocktail is the winter holidays. My wife's favorite holiday martini is a chocolate martini, and I love the use of a classic Hershey's Kiss in the bottom of the glass. Using the chocolate martini as inspiration, I wanted to create a drink that would use a candy found everywhere during Christmas time—the candy cane. What started as a simple vodka martini got elevated at Market in Rocky River with the addition of Godiva White Chocolate. This masterpiece became the signature drink for my wife's 50th birthday party. It's tasty and so simple, but it is a guaranteed show-stopper at your holiday party.

You Will Need:
1 oz Pope's Mint Cocktail Syrup
3 oz Godiva White Chocolate Liqueur
3 oz vodka
2 teaspoons crushed peppermints or candy cane
1 oz heavy cream
2 cups of ice, divided

Tools & Glassware:
2 rocks or martini glasses
Hawthorne strainer
Shaker set*

Garnish:
Mini candy canes

Method:
1. Pre-chill the martini glass by filling with ice while preparing the drink.
2. Measure liquids into your shaker.
3. Add the candy cane into the shaker.
4. Add half your ice to the shaker*.
5. Shake until a light frost forms on the tin—roughly a 10 to 15 count
6. Discard the ice from the pre-chilled glasses.
7. Strain a little into each glass at a time so that they both end with a light foam on top.
8. Garnish the glasses with a mini candy cane.

Make it your own! Notes...

Alternatives
Swap out the White Godiva for crème de coco
Swap out the heavy cream for an egg white for more foam

Personal Tweaks

I should drink this with...

POPE'S GLACIER

My daughter asked me to create a cocktail to celebrate the family glacier named for my cousin, Retired Lieutenant Colonel Donald R. Pope U.S. Army Corps of Engineers, for his work with the Naval Support Force, Antarctica. As a toast to Don and all those who have served in Antarctica, here is a liquid Glacier, served in a chilled glass, a blend of white chocolate, vodka and the Pope's Orange Vanilla Cocktail Syrup

You Will Need:

1.5 oz Pope's Orange Vanilla Cocktail Syrup
3 oz vodka
2 oz white chocolate liqueur
2 cups of ice, divided

Tools & Glassware:

2 martini glasses
Shaker set
Jigger

Garnish:

Orange twist
Powdered sugar to rim

Method:

1. Pre-chill glassware by dividing half of the ice into each glass.
2. Add remaining ice to the shaker*.
3. Add Pope's Orange Vanilla Cocktail Syrup, chocolate liqueur, and vodka to the shaker.
4. Shake until a light frost forms on the tin – roughly a 10 to 15 count.
5. Discard the ice from pre-chilling the glasses.
6. Strain beverage into the glasses.
7. Garnish the glasses with orange twist, cut the rind off the slice, grip in both hands and twist.
8. For effect, rub the rim and top inch of the glass with the orange slice, dust with powdered sugar.

*Don't have a shaker set? Roll the cocktail with half the ice between two pint glasses four times, then strain, garnish and serve.

Make it your own! Notes...

Alternatives

Replace white chocolate liqueur with a coffee liqueur.

Personal Tweaks

I should drink this with...

PUMPKIN PIE MARTINI

Nothing says fall like the inviting aroma of a freshly baked pumpkin pie. Honestly my pie baking skills are not what they could be, so I devised a liquid version.

You Will Need:

2 oz Pope's Pumpkin Spice Cocktail Syrup
3 oz vodka
2 oz Irish cream liqueur
2 cups of ice, divided

Tools & Glassware:

2 Martini glasses
Shaker set
Jigger
Hawthorne strainer

Garnish:

Fresh nutmeg
Orange twist

Method:

1. Pre-chill your glassware by dividing half of the ice into each glass.
2. Add remaining ice to the shaker*.
3. Add Pope's Pumpkin Spice Cocktail Syrup, Irish cream liqueur, and vodka to the shaker.
4. Shake until a light frost forms on the tin – roughly a 10 to 15 count.
5. Discard the ice from pre-chilling the glasses.
6. Strain beverage into the glasses.
7. Garnish the glasses with orange twist and lightly dust the top of the drinks with fresh nutmeg.

*Don't have a shaker set? Roll the cocktail with half the ice between two pint glasses four times, then strain, garnish and serve.

Make it your own! Notes...

Alternatives

Replace vodka with bourbon.
Replace Irish cream with chocolate liqueur

Personal Tweaks

I should drink this with...

SPA TREATMENT

Inspired by the dog days of summer, Spa Treatment is a clean and cool cocktail that refreshes the palate and the soul. While extremely easy to execute, this drink is sophisticated in delivery. Minimalist in nature, the light mint flavor and mild character of this cocktail are reminiscent of mineral water drinks served in classy spas. It's excellent served on its own, particularly outdoors, this cocktail is also a post-meal favorite.

My friend, Ryan Oldham of Make It Fancy Cocktails, penned the above description of Spa Treatment. It was an awesome surprise to check out Instagram and find this beautiful cocktail, and Ryan was kind enough to share it with me. Check out Make It Fancy Cocktails on Instagram.

You Will Need:
0.5 oz Pope's Mint Cocktail Syrup
2 oz premium vodka
Seltzer water
Ice cubes

Tools & Glassware:
Collins glass
Bar spoon

Garnish:
Lime or cucumber wheel

Method:
1. Build the beverage directly in glass.
2. Fill glass ¾ with ice.
3. Pour Pope's Mint Cocktail Syrup and vodka over ice.
4. Stir gently with bar spoon.
5. Pour seltzer water into glass, leaving about an inch of space below the rim.
6. Stir again, gently.
7. Run garnish around the rim of the glass. Place garnish on rim.

Make it your own! Notes...

Alternatives
Double the amount Pope's Mint Cocktail Syrup for a cooler mint character
Add a squeeze of fresh lime juice to brighten up the acidity.

Personal Tweaks

I should drink this with...

THE BASIC

Basic… This term is often meant to be an insult, which somehow, I never understood. You can hide a lot of faults in a complex cocktail, so keep it simple and keep it clean. For example, here we have four of the most basic building blocks of flavor, and yet, when combined, we create a multi-layered cocktail with a rich texture. It goes to show that you don't have to be a complex to be great. You just need to be you.

You Will Need:

- 1.5 oz. Pope's Pumpkin Spice Cocktail Syrup
- 3 oz. vodka
- 2 oz. chocolate liqueur
- 2 oz. heavy cream
- 1 cup of ice, divided

Tools & Glassware:

- 2 rocks glasses
- Jigger
- Bar spoon
- Shaker set*

Garnish:

Chocolate sauce

Method:

1. Divide half the ice into each glass.
2. Add remaining ice to the shaker*.
3. Add Pope's Pumpkin Spice Cocktail Syrup, chocolate liqueur, heavy cream, and vodka to the shaker.
4. Shake until a light frost forms on the tin – roughly a 10 to 15 count.
5. Strain beverage into rocks glasses over ice, dividing evenly between glasses. Add ice if needed.
6. Garnish with a drizzle of chocolate sauce.

*Don't have a shaker set? Roll the cocktail with half the ice between two pint glasses four times, then strain, garnish and serve.

Make it your own! Notes…

Alternatives

Replace vodka with bourbon

Personal Tweaks

I should drink this with…

THYME FOR BLUEBERRY

Some flavors belong together, and at the height of blueberry season, fresh blueberry scones with thyme butter is a perfect treat for high tea in Great Britain. The American version of the tea time is the cocktail hour, and I highly recommend spending a summer afternoon sipping on this drink the next time you partake in the cocktail hour.

You Will Need:

1.5 oz Pope's Blueberry Lemon
3 oz gin or vodka
2 oz club soda
2 sprigs of thyme, leaves stripped
2 cups of ice, divided

Tools & Glassware:

2 Collins glasses
Hawthorne strainer
Shaker set*

Garnish:

Spring of thyme
Fresh blueberries

Method:

1. Measure the cocktail syrup and gin into your shaker.
2. Add stripped thyme leaves.
3. Add half the ice to the shaker*.
4. Distribute the remaining ice evenly among two Collins glasses.
5. Shake until a light frost forms on the tin – roughly a 10 to 15 count.
6. Add club soda to the shaker.
7. Strain into Collins glasses, filling half into each glass then topping off.
8. Garnish the glasses with spring of thyme and blueberries.

* Don't have a shaker set? Roll the cocktail with half the ice between two pint glasses four times, and then strain into the correct glassware, garnish and serve.

Make it your own! Notes...

Alternatives

Swap out club soda for Sprite.
Swap out the thyme leaves for basil leaves.

Personal Tweaks

I should drink this with...

DIRTY IS GOOD

While the martini may be enjoyed by smartly dressed spies the world over, it is the lust-filled gaze on a cloudy, shimmering, cold dirty martini that truly sets the stage for intrigue. Why do I shake and not stir a dirty martini? I think that the colder the drink, the crisper the layers of flavor are. By shaking the drink, small flecks of ice will pour into the glass, helping to keep the drink chilled, and adding a slight amount of dilution as they melt.

You Will Need:
1.5 oz Pope's Dirty Martini Blend
5 oz dry gin
1 oz dry vermouth
2 cups of ice, divided

Tools & Glassware:
2 martini glasses
Hawthorne strainer
Shaker set*
Jigger

Garnish:
Olives
Lemon wheel or twist

Method:
1. Properly chill your glassware by dividing half of the ice into each glass.
2. Add remaining ice to the shaker*.
3. Add gin, vermouth, and Pope's Dirty Martini Blend to the shaker.
4. Shake until a light frost forms on the tin – roughly a 10 to 15 count.
5. Discard the ice from pre-chilling the martini glasses.
6. Strain the drink into the martini glasses.
7. Garnish the glasses with olives and a lemon wheel or twist

* Don't have a shaker set? Don't believe in shaking a martini? Use a pint glass or Yarai glass, and stir the drink using and a bar spoon. Let the glass rest when the liquid settles, then strain into the martini glasses, garnish and serve.

Make it your own! Notes...

Alternatives
Swap out vodka for gin.
Use bleu cheese stuffed olives.

Personal Tweaks

I should drink this with...

GIN AND JUICE

Mid-September was the first annual Bartenders Island Getaway at Put In Bay island in Lake Erie. This year we gathered 55 bartenders and United States Bartender's Guild members from around the country for two days of social events and relaxation. For our put-put game, several of us created cocktails and obstacles to entice and challenge the golfers. To offset the humidity, I took first place with a refreshing glass of orange juice, with a splash of gin and a touch of the Pope's Orange Habanero Cocktail Syrup.

You Will Need:
1.5 oz Pope's Orange Habanero
4 oz dry gin
5 oz orange juice
2 cups of ice, divided

Tools & Glassware:
2 rocks glasses
Hawthorne strainer
Shaker set*
Jigger

Garnish:
Orange wheel or twist

Method:
1. Measure the Pope's Cocktail Syrup, Gin and orange juice into the shaker.
2. Add half the ice to the shaker*.
3. Distribute the remaining ice evenly among two rocks glasses.
4. Shake until a light frost forms on the tin – roughly a 10 to 15 count.
5. Strain into rocks glasses,
6. Garnish the glasses with a twist of orange

* Don't have a shaker set? Roll the cocktail with half the ice between two pint glasses four times, and then strain into the correct glassware, garnish and serve.

Make it your own! Notes...

Alternatives
Swap out vodka for gin.
Use bleu cheese stuffed olives.

Personal Tweaks

I should drink this with...

GIN FLING

It's always fun to collaborate with small businesses. My friends at Inca Tea serve a wonderful Spiced Berry Tea, and when they opened their first café with a full bar, I designed a few drinks using Pope's Cocktail Syrups to highlight their teas. I created a delicious cocktail that blends the Spiced Berry Tea with Watershed Distillery's Four Peel Gin and Pope's Lavender Lemon Cocktail. Enjoy this cocktail with your friends and see if you can pick out all of the flavors.

You Will Need:

1.5 oz Pope's Lavender Lemon Syrup
6 oz Spiced Berry Tea, Inca Tea
3 oz Watershed Distillery Four Peel Gin
2 cups of ice, divided

Tools & Glassware:

2 rocks glasses
Shaker Set
Jigger

Garnish:

Lemon Wheel

Method:

1. Pour Pope's Lavender Lemon Cocktail Syrup, tea, and gin into the shaker.
2. Add half the ice to the shaker*.
3. Distribute the remaining ice evenly among two rocks glasses.
4. Shake until a light frost forms on the tin – roughly a 10 to 15 count.
5. Strain beverage into rocks glasses, filling half into each then topping off.
6. Garnish the glasses with lemon wheel.

* Don't have a shaker set? Roll the cocktail with half the ice between two pint glasses four times, and then strain into the correct glassware, garnish and serve.

Make it your own! Notes...

Alternatives

Use frozen raspberries to garnish.

Personal Tweaks

I should drink this with...

LAVENDER GIN-GINGER PUNCH

Growing up, every church function had the same punch – a concoction of ginger ale and white grape juice. It has a great sparkle from the soda, and the tartness of the grape juice cuts the sweetness of the ginger ale. These days, I have dressed it up a bit by adding Pope's Lavender Lemon Cocktail Syrup to balance it with a floral note. When serving punch for grownups, I spike it with an American-style gin (more citrus and floral notes and less juniper). This punch is great for a spring or summer party. Without the gin, this is a great punch for baby showers.

You Will Need:
4 oz Pope's Lavender Lemon Syrup
8 oz American-style gin
2 cups white grape juice
2 cups ginger ale

Tools & Glassware:
Half-gallon pitcher or punch bowl
Bar spoon
Jigger

Garnish:
Frozen mixed berries

Method:
1. Pre-chill the liquids before mixing.
2. Gently pour pre-chilled white grape juice and gin into the pitcher or punch bowl.
3. Turn the spoon upside down and pour the Pope's Lavender Lemon Cocktail Syrup over it.
4. Use the spoon to stir briskly to combine.
5. Just before serving, add the pre-chilled ginger ale and stir gently to combine.
6. Float the frozen berries to keep punch cold. This also adds nice color.
7. Allow guests to help themselves
8. Garnish the glasses with fresh or frozen berries.

Make it your own! Notes...

Alternatives
Leave out the gin.
Replace half the ginger ale with ginger beer.

Personal Tweaks

I should drink this with...

LAVENDER LEMON SPRITZ

I will never forget the day I met Nicki Moore from Watershed Distillery. She moved with such intense energy and belief in her products. I had not tasted gin in years, but there was no resisting a clear direction to try the Four Peel Gin, and I was instantly made into a true believer. As we had opportunities to work on projects together, Pope's Lavender Lemon Cocktail Syrup was developed, forming a perfect pairing, in which the soft floral notes of organic lavender and lemon in a rich simple syrup blends with a complex, citrus-forward gin.

As my dear friend Nicki would put it – The Watershed Four Peel Gin is "wonderfully citrus-forward with a lower juniper content than most London dry styles. With cinnamon, coriander, and allspice lingering in the background, the Lavender Lemon Syrup offers a burst of floral flavor, while the lemon accentuates the citrus. It goes down even easier than a classic Tom Collins. We promise, this is the easiest drinking gin cocktail you'll have all summer."

You Will Need:

1.5 oz Pope's Lavender Lemon Syrup
3 oz Watershed Four Peel Gin
6 oz Club soda
2 cups of ice, divided

Tools & Glassware:

2 Collins glasses
Bar spoon
Jigger

Garnish:

Lemon wheel
Edible flower

Method:

1. Build drink directly in each glass.
2. Fill each glass with ice.
3. Pour Pope's Lavender Lemon Cocktail Syrup and gin into each glass over the ice.
4. Gently stir to combine.
5. Top with club soda and stir three times.
6. Garnish the glasses with lemon wheel and edible flower.

Make it your own! Notes...

Alternatives
Makes for an equally delicious Vodka Collins with Watershed Vodka

Personal Tweaks

I should drink this with...

HAIR CUT

My friend Nancy has so much passion for a fine cocktail that she joined the United States Bartenders' Guild as a non-bartender enthusiast, and then stepped up into a leadership position as a membership co-chair to get others to come celebrate her passion with her. When the call went out to contribute to this book, Nancy responded instantly.

You Will Need:

1 oz Pope's Orange Habanero Cocktail Syrup
4 oz gin (Nancy likes Botanist for this)
3 oz dry vermouth
1 dash of orange bitters
1 cup of ice, divided

Tools & Glassware:

2 rocks glasses
Bar spoon

Garnish:

Orange twist

Method:

1. Build in the rocks glass, dividing ice between each glass.
2. Pour Pope's Orange Habanero Cocktail Syrup, gin and vermouth over ice
3. Add a dash of orange bitters
4. Garnish the glasses with an orange twist

Make it your own! Notes...

Alternatives
Use one large ice cube, per glass

Personal Tweaks

I should drink this with...

A MIDNIGHT STORM

In my opinion, the best opening line ever is "it was a dark and stormy night…" I truly believe that it is this line that gives us the classic rum and ginger beer cocktail. Taking inspiration from this ominous opening line, I re-imagined this cocktail by adding Pope's Blueberry Lemon Cocktail Syrup, and changing the dark rum to spiced rum. Just as the suspense of a dark and stormy night fuels curiosity, adding my cocktail syrup to this drink creates the rich, dark purple hue of midnight that compels you to taste. Best enjoyed watching a rainstorm on a summer's evening or during an afternoon on the water.

You Will Need:

1.5 oz Pope's Blueberry Lemon Syrup
3 oz spiced rum
6 oz ginger beer
2 cups of ice, divided

Tools & Glassware:

2 rocks glasses
Bar spoon

Garnish:

Lime wheel
Fresh blueberries

Method:

1. Build the beverage directly in rocks glasses.
2. Distribute ice evenly among glasses.
3. Add rum to ice.
4. Pour Pope's Cocktail Syrup into rum.
5. Stir to combine, then add ginger beer.
6. Stir again, gently.
7. Garnish with lime wheel and blueberries.

Make it your own! Notes...

Alternatives

Too spicy? Swap ginger beer for Sprite.

Personal Tweaks

I should drink this with...

A PIRATE'S PUMPKIN

What's a pirate's favorite sock? Arrrr-gyle! As the summer breaks to fall, even the pirates look to the creamy richness of pumpkins to accent their Rum. I always recommend Spiced Rum when dealing with pirates and a touch of citrus to prevent scurvy.

You Will Need:
1.5 oz Pope's Pumpkin Spice Cocktail Syrup
3 oz spiced rum
1 oz orange juice
2 cups of ice, divided

Tools & Glassware:
2 rocks glasses
Shaker*
Jigger
Hawthorn strainer

Garnish:
Orange slice
Fresh ground nutmeg

Method:
1. Measure Pope's Pumpkin Spice Cocktail Syrup, Rum, and orange juice into the shaker.
2. Add half the ice to the shaker*.
3. Distribute the remaining ice evenly among two rocks glasses.
4. Shake until a light frost forms on the tin – roughly a 10 to 15 count.
5. Strain into rocks glasses, filling half into each then topping off.
6. Garnish the glasses with orange slice and fresh nutmeg.

* Don't have a shaker set? Roll the cocktail with half the ice between two pint glasses four times, and then strain into the correct glassware, garnish and serve.

Make it your own! Notes...

Alternatives
Replace the orange juice with lemon juice
For land pirates, use bourbon.

Personal Tweaks

I should drink this with...

CLASSIC MOJITO

For me, nothing heralds the approach of warm weather like the smell of mint. Add to it a little rum, and it's the perfect summer day. Science supports this! Research conducted at the University of Cincinnati finds that "mint...increases the oxygen count in your blood, increasing the flow to your brain causing you to be more attentive." Thus, Mojitos make you more focused, which in turn lets you enjoy your day even more. Here, I make the perfect Mojito by taking away the work of muddling the mint and sugar. Try this once and I promise you will have again.

You Will Need:
2 oz Pope's Mint Cocktail Syrup
4 oz white rum
2 oz club soda
4 lime wedges
2 cups of ice, divided

Tools & Glassware:
2 Collins Glasses 10 - 12 oz.
Shaker set*
Jigger

Garnish:
Wedge of lime
Sprig of fresh mint

Method:
1. Add half your ice to the shaker*.
2. Measure Pope's Mint Cocktail Syrup and rum into the shaker.
3. Squeeze lime wedges into the shaker and drop them into the tin.
4. Shake until a light frost forms on the tin – roughly a 10 to 15 count.
5. Add club soda to the shaker.
6. Pour beverage, making sure the lime wedges get into each glass.
7. Add additional ice to fill the glass as needed.
8. Garnish the glasses with spring of mint and lime wedge

* Don't have a shaker set? Roll the cocktail with half the ice between two pint glasses four times, and then pour into the correct glassware, garnish and serve.

Make it your own! Notes...

Alternatives
Swap out soda water for Sprite
Try using .5 oz Pope's Mint and 1 oz Pope's Blueberry Syrup

Personal Tweaks

I should drink this with...

FALL HARVEST

I think it is fair to say that all of my family traditions center around food. Growing up, each fall we would go to Toledo to see my grandparents and go apple picking with my grandfather for his birthday. He liked to pick the ones that had fallen from the tree and make apple cider or apple sauce. In this drink, I join fresh apple cider with another fall favorite, pumpkin pie.

You Will Need:

1.5 oz Pope's Pumpkin Spice Cocktail Syrup
3 oz spiced rum
4 oz apple cider
2 cups of ice, divided

Tools & Glassware:

2 rocks glasses
Shaker set
Jigger
Hawthorne strainer

Garnish:

Thin apple slice

Method:

1. Divide half of the ice among each glass.
2. Add remaining ice to the shaker*.
3. Add Pope's Pumpkin Spice Cocktail Syrup, apple cider, and rum to the shaker.
4. Shake until a light frost forms on the tin – roughly a 10 to 15 count.
5. Strain beverage into the rocks glasses.
6. Garnish the glasses with an apple slice.

*Don't have a shaker set? Roll the cocktail with half the ice between two pint glasses four times, then strain, garnish and serve.

Make it your own! Notes...

Alternatives

Replace rum with bourbon.

Personal Tweaks

I should drink this with...

ORANGE YOU GLAD

Knock, knock. Who's there? Banana. Banana Who? Knock, knock… and the joke goes on. Here, you can have the last laugh with a jovial blend of Pope's Orange Vanilla Cocktail Syrup, orange juice, and spiced rum.

You Will Need:

1.5 oz Pope's Orange Vanilla Cocktail Syrup
3 oz spiced rum
2 oz orange juice
1 cup of ice

Tools & Glassware:

2 rocks glasses
Shaker Set
Jigger
Hawthorne Strainer

Garnish:

Orange slice

Method:

1. Add ice to the shaker*.
2. Add Pope's Orange Vanilla Cocktail Syrup, orange juice, and Spiced Rum to the shaker.
3. Shake until a light frost forms on the tin – roughly a 10 to 15 count.
4. Pour into the rocks glasses, making sure to get a bit of ice into each one. Add more ice as needed.
5. Garnish the glasses with an orange slice.

*Don't have a shaker set? Roll the cocktail with half the ice between two pint glasses four times, then strain, garnish and serve.

Make it your own! Notes...

Alternatives

Replace the Orange Vanilla Syrup with Pope's Orange Habanero Cocktail Syrup.
Replace the rum with vodka.

Personal Tweaks

I should drink this with...

POPE'S ISLAND TEA

I dream of one day retiring, moving to a beach or small island somewhere warm, and opening a small brunch place. I'd serve brunch from 11-3 and then have a nap on the beach. Between now and retirement, there will always be boat drinks, and here is a personal favorite of mine.

You Will Need:

1.5 oz Pope's Orange Vanilla Cocktail Syrup
1.5 oz whiskey
1.5 oz tequila
1.5 oz rum
1 cup of ice, divided

Tools & Glassware:

2 Collins glasses
Bar spoon
Jigger

Garnish:

Lemon
Coca-Cola

Method:

1. Build drink directly in glasses.
2. Divide half of the ice into each glass.
3. Pour the rum, whiskey, and tequila over ice.
4. Add Pope's Orange Vanilla Cocktail Syrup.
5. Gently stir to combine.
6. Garnish the glasses by topping off with Coke and a squeeze of lemon, and serve with a straw.

Make it your own! Notes...

Alternatives

Replace the Orange Vanilla Syrup with Pope's Orange Habanero Cocktail Syrup.
Replace Coke with orange juice.

Personal Tweaks

I should drink this with...

SPRING FLING

Ah…springtime in Cleveland… Those two weeks from the melting of the snow to the arrival of 80 degree days. If you watch carefully, you can see the planting of the famous orange barrel flowers along the roads. So, to celebrate this brief relationship, I give you the Spring Fling—a touch of springtime mint and the passionate heat of a habanero. Enjoy whenever you feel your heart flutter at a new beginning.

You Will Need:

.5 oz Pope's Mint Cocktail Syrup
1 oz Pope's Orange Habanero Syrup
3 oz Spiced Rum
2 cups of ice, divided

Tools & Glassware:

2 rocks glasses
Hawthorne strainer
Shaker set*
Jigger

Garnish:

Fresh mint

Method:

1. Measure the Pope's Cocktail Syrups and Spiced Rum into the shaker.
2. Add half the ice to the shaker*.
3. Distribute the remaining ice evenly among two rocks glasses.
4. Shake until a light frost forms on the tin – roughly a 10 to 15 count.
5. Strain into rocks glasses, filling half into each then topping off.
6. Garnish the glasses with mint

* Don't have a shaker set? Roll the cocktail with half the ice between two pint glasses four times, and then pour into the correct glassware, garnish and serve.

Make it your own! Notes…

Alternatives
Add a splash of fresh lemon juice

Personal Tweaks

I should drink this with…

POPE LOOKS AT 45

I have an unabashed love for Jimmy Buffet. The music is uncomplicated and does not pretend to be anything other than what it is—relaxing rhythms with solid storytelling. Like many others, I have always enjoyed the self-reflection of "A Pirate Looks at 40," which is strange as he was 28 when it was recorded. At 53, Jimmy released "A Pirate Looks at 50," a collection of personal reflections. Now that I am 46, I give you my reflections in a glass. Life cannot be all beaches (rum & lime) or all business (bourbon); there has to be a balance.

You Will Need:

1.5 oz Pope's Mint Cocktail Syrup
4 oz Kentucky bourbon
1 oz fresh lime juice
2 oz club soda (optional)
2 cups of ice, divided

Tools & Glassware:

2 Collins glasses, 10 - 12 oz.
Shaker set*
Jigger

Garnish:

Fresh mint
Half of a lime wheel

Method:

1. Measure the Pope's Mint Cocktail Syrup, bourbon, and lime juice into the shaker.
2. Add half the ice to the shaker*.
3. Shake until a light frost forms on the tin – roughly a 10 to 15 count.
4. Add club soda to the shaker.
5. Pour beverage into each glass.
6. Add remaining ice to fill each glass as needed.
7. Garnish the glasses with spring of mint and lime wheel.

* Don't have a shaker set? Roll the cocktail with half the ice between two pint glasses four times, and then pour into the correct glassware, garnish and serve.

Make it your own! Notes...

Alternatives

Swap out club soda for Sprite
Drink in a hammock

Personal Tweaks

I should drink this with...

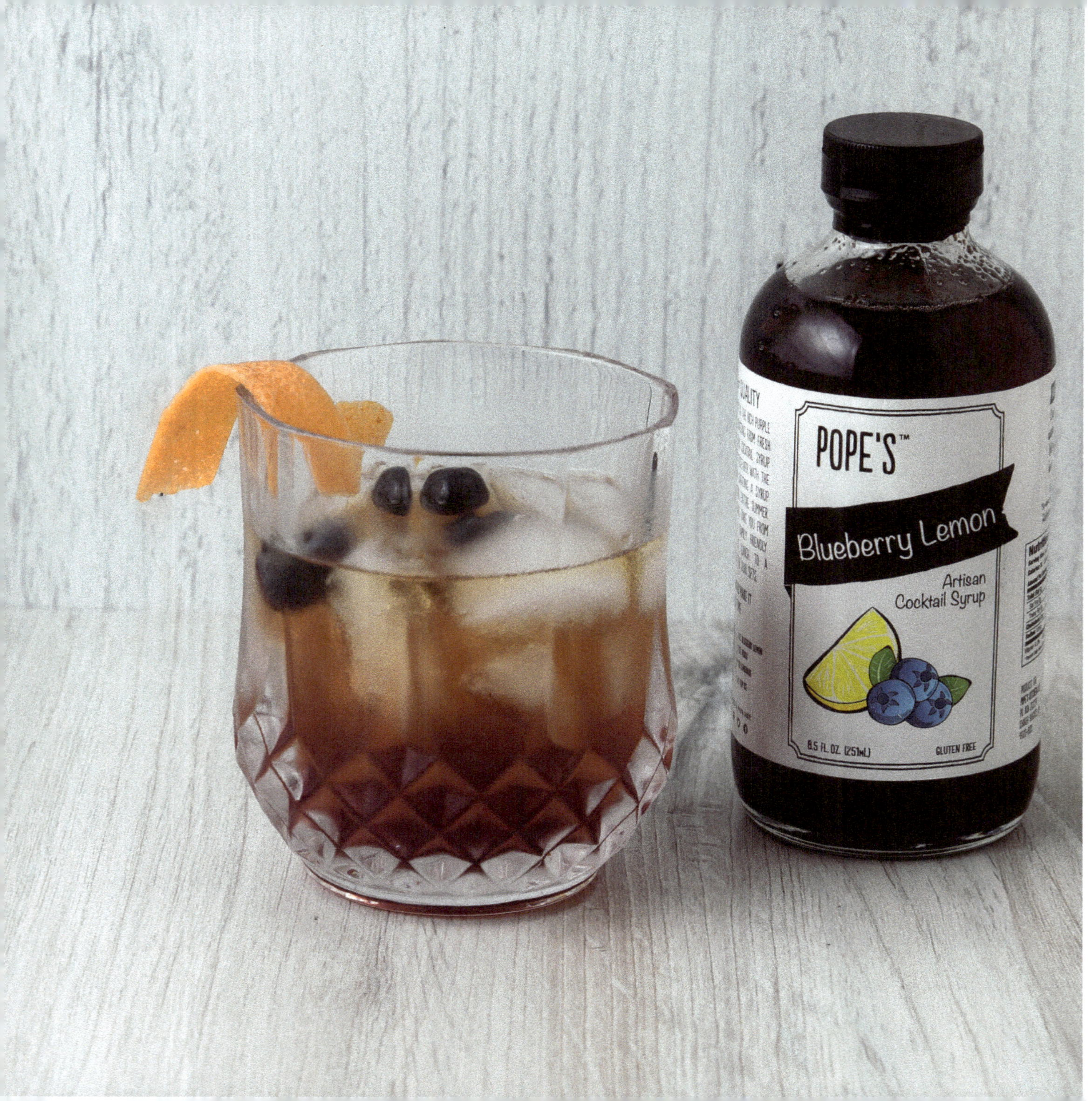
POPE'S™
Blueberry Lemon
Artisan
Cocktail Syrup
8.5 FL. OZ. (251mL)
GLUTEN FREE

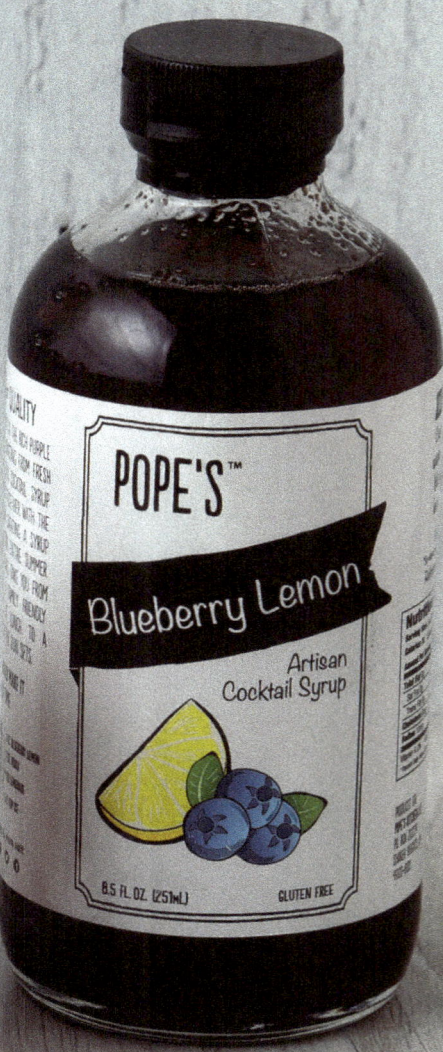

BLUEBERRY OLD FASHIONED

The creation of the Old Fashioned hearkens back to the late 1800s in Louisville, Kentucky. Because of this cocktail's staying power and mass appeal, the city declared the Old Fashioned its official cocktail in 2015. It is a very simple concoction of bourbon, Angostura bitters, a sugar cube, a splash of water, and garnished with an orange peel and cherry. I, however, have more than just a bit of a sweet tooth and a need for flavor. I prefer to replace the sugar cube with a splash of my Blueberry Lemon Cocktail Syrup.

You Will Need:
5 oz Bourbon
2 oz Pope's Blueberry Lemon Cocktail Syrup
A dash of Angostura bitters
2 cups of ice, divided

Tools & Glassware:
2 rocks glasses
Bar spoon
Jigger

Garnish:
Fresh blueberries

Method:
1. Build the beverage directly in rocks glasses.
2. Distribute ice evenly between the glasses.
3. Add bourbon to ice.
4. Pour Pope's Blueberry Lemon Cocktail Syrup into glass, top with bitters and stir to combine.
5. Garnish with fresh blueberries.

Make it your own! Notes...

Alternatives
Too strong? Add a splash of cold water.

Personal Tweaks

I should drink this with...

KENTUCKY BLUES

2nd Place – Winner for the Ezra Brooks Bourbon Competition

In celebration of my Kentucky roots, and memories of spending early mornings at the Kentucky Farm Park seeing the dew give the grass a soft blue hue, I decided to pay homage to my home state by creating a blueberry mint smash with bourbon. It is the perfect cocktail for savoring at the end of the day. This was my very first competition cocktail, and I was pleasantly surprised to have garnered second place amongst a field of very talented bartenders.

You Will Need:
1 oz Pope's Blueberry Lemon Syrup
.5 oz Pope's Mint Syrup
4 oz bourbon
2 cups of ice, divided
2 oz club soda

Tools & Glassware:
2 rocks glasses
Hawthorne strainer
Shaker set*
Jigger

Garnish:
Fresh mint
Fresh blueberries

Method:
1. Measure the cocktail syrups and bourbon into your shaker.
2. Add half the ice to the shaker*.
3. Distribute the remaining ice evenly among two rocks glasses.
4. Shake until a light frost forms on the tin – roughly a 10 to 15 count.
5. Add club soda to the tin, and strain into rocks glasses, filling half into each glass then topping off.
6. Garnish the glasses with fresh mint and blueberries.

* Don't have a shaker set? Roll the cocktail with half the ice between two pint glasses four times, and then strain into the correct glassware, garnish, and serve.

Make it your own! Notes...

Alternatives
Swap out club soda for Sprite.

Personal Tweaks

I should drink this with...

POPE'S FAMILY MINT JULEP

As of 2019, the first Saturday in May has seen the running of the Kentucky Derby for 144 years. That is a claim of tradition, nearly unmatched in this country. Like all great traditions, it brings people together and it includes its very own drink—the mint julep. This drink has a recorded history in the U.S. that dates back to before 1850. Part of the mystique of the mint julep is its vessel. It is a sterling silver or pewter cup, filled with crushed ice, so that the thermal property of the metal transfers the heat from your hand and melts the ice, which blends the drink as you socialize. For the Pope family, the Mint Julep is built with a handmade simple syrup, fresh mint, and Kentucky Bourbon, and served freely to friends and family alike. Here is the Pope family recipe. Enjoy with your friends and continue the tradition.

You Will Need:

2 oz Pope's Mint Cocktail Syrup
5 oz bourbon
2 Cups of Crushed Ice, Divided

Tools & Glassware:

2 silver julep cups or rocks glassed
Jigger

Garnish:

2 sprigs fresh mint

Method:

1. Fill each cup with crushed ice.
2. Pour Pope's Mint Cocktail Syrup over the ice.
3. Add the bourbon.
4. Garnish with a spring of mint to each cup.

Make it your own! Notes...

Alternatives

Splash of club soda to top
Official Derby glass

Personal Tweaks

I should drink this with...

THE POPE OF SLAVIC VILLAGE

One of the greatest joys of creating products is to see how other people make use of them. One of our great partners is a new distillery in Lakewood Ohio. Opened in 2018, Western Reserve Distillery is one of three certified organic distilleries in the United States. If you find yourself in Lakewood, stop by and taste their selection of organic Gin, Vodka, Rum, and Bourbon. Their master of the bar, Tim Harnett, shares this recipe with us.

You Will Need:
2 oz Pope's Orange Habanero Syrup
7 oz Thai restaurant-style tea
3 oz Western Reserve Distillery Bourbon
3 oz half and half
2 cups of ice, divided

Tools & Glassware:
2 large rocks glasses
Hawthorne strainer
Shaker set
Jigger

Garnish:
Slice of red jalapeno

Method:
1. Add half the ice to the shaker*.
2. Pour Pope's Orange Habanero Cocktail Syrup, tea, and Western Reserve Bourbon into the tin.
3. Shake until a light frost forms on the tin – roughly a 10 to 15 count.
4. Check to make sure the cream is incorporated.
5. Strain into each glass, a little at a time so that they both end with light foam on top.
6. Garnish by laying the red jalapeno across the top of each glass.

Make it your own! Notes...

Alternatives
Earl Grey tea
Slice of orange for garnish

Personal Tweaks

I should drink this with...

THE BIG PEACH

Peaches, rye whiskey, and mint…I think I can stop here? Warm peach pie and a cold drink, what else is heaven made from? Life is full of big questions, but maybe we can let some slide and just enjoy a nice drink.

You Will Need:

1 oz Pope's Mint Cocktail Syrup
6 oz Inca Tea peach kombucha,
3 oz Cleveland Underground Rye Whiskey
2 cups of ice, divided

Tools & Glassware:

2 rocks glasses
Shaker*
Jigger

Garnish:

Fresh Mint
Fresh peach slice

Method:

1. Measure the Pope's Mint Cocktail Syrup, kombucha, and Rye Whiskey into the shaker.
2. Add half the ice to the shaker*.
3. Distribute the remaining ice evenly among two rocks glasses.
4. Shake until a light frost forms on the tin – roughly a 10 to 15 count.
5. Strain into rocks glasses, filling half into each then topping off.
6. Garnish the glasses with a slice of peach and mint

* Don't have a shaker set? Roll the cocktail with half the ice between two pint glasses four times, and then strain into the correct glassware, garnish and serve.

Make it your own! Notes...

Alternatives

Use frozen peaches as half the ice
Muddle 1 peach slice in the glass

Personal Tweaks

I should drink this with...

MY LAST NIGHT IN TIJUANA

I was asked to take part in a cocktail competition at a local bar, and I was told to use Tequila. I had just finished developing the Dirty Martini Blend, and I knew I wanted to feature it. I went to bed thinking I needed something more than a dirty tequila martini, and of all of the fun ways I could do this. As I laid there, I remembered a family trip to Tijuana and all of the intense sights and sounds. I also remembered how poor my Spanish was, and while at a bar, I ordered what I thought was a spicy orange soda, but instead was a spiced tequila drink. The memory of my mistranslation inspired this delightfully salty, spicy martini.

You Will Need:
1.5 oz Pope's Orange Habanero Syrup
1 oz Pope's Dirty Martini Blend
5 oz blanco tequila
2 cups of ice, divided

Tools & Glassware:
2 martini glasses
Hawthorne strainer
Shaker set*
Jigger

Garnish:
Half lime wheel
Spiced salt rim

Method:
1. Add half the ice to the shaker*.
2. Measure Pope's Dirty Martini Blend, Orange Habanero Syrup and tequila into the shaker.
3. Distribute the remaining ice evenly among two martini glasses.
4. Shake until a light frost forms on the tin – roughly a 10 to 15 count.
5. Discard ice from martini glasses and rim with salt if desired.
6. Strain the drink into the martini glasses, filling half into each then topping off.
7. Garnish the glasses with lime wheel.

* Don't have a shaker set? Roll the cocktail with half the ice between two pint glasses four times, and then strain into the correct glassware, garnish, and serve.

Make it your own! Notes...

Alternatives
Try with mescal

Personal Tweaks

I should drink this with...

ORANGE VANILLA MARGARITA

A classic like the margarita rarely needs to be improved upon. Yet, I must say, that an addition of the sweet floral notes of a vanilla bean really open this drink up to be truly celebrated. Save your blender for morning smoothies because this is all about the rocks.

You Will Need:

2 oz Pope's Orange Vanilla Cocktail Syrup
3 oz aged tequila
1 oz orange juice
1 oz lemon juice
1 oz lime juice
2 cups of ice, divided

Tools & Glassware:

2 rocks glasses
Shaker set
Jigger
Hawthorne strainer

Garnish:

Orange slice
Salt to rim, optional

Method:

1. Add salt to rim of the glasses, if using, and divide half the ice into each glass.
2. Add remaining ice to the shaker*.
3. Add Pope's Orange Vanilla Cocktail Syrup, juices, and tequila to the shaker.
4. Shake until a light frost forms on the tin – roughly a 10 to 15 count.
5. Strain beverage into the rocks glasses.
6. Garnish the glasses with orange slice.

*Don't have a shaker set? Roll the cocktail with half the ice between two pint glasses four times, then strain, garnish and serve.

Make it your own! Notes...

Alternatives

Replace the Orange Vanilla Syrup with Pope's Orange Habanero Cocktail Syrup.
Replace the tequila with rum.

Personal Tweaks

I should drink this with...

SPICY PALOMA

Competition Cocktail - Second Place Qualifying Round Extinguish Cocktail Competition, 2019

I created this with a nod to a classic tequila cocktail, the Paloma, which is created from grapefruit soda and tequila. The switch from bottled soda to fresh grapefruit provides a tart contrast to the Pope's Orange Habanero Syrup. Much like the contrast between the current reborn healthy Cuyahoga River and the great fire of 1969.

You Will Need:

1.5 oz Pope's Orange Habanero Syrup
4 oz Cantera Negra Reposado Tequila
3 oz fresh grapefruit juice
1 oz fresh lime juice
2 cups of ice, divided
Splash of club soda

Tools & Glassware:

Rocks glasses
Hawthorne strainer
Shaker set*
Jigger

Garnish:

Half of a lime wheel

Method:

1. Measure Pope's Orange Habanero Cocktail Syrup, grapefruit juice, lime juice, and tequila into the shaker.
2. Add half the ice to the shaker*.
3. Distribute the remaining ice evenly among two rocks glasses.
4. Shake until a light frost forms on the tin – roughly a 10 to 15 count.
5. Add a splash of club soda directly to the tin.
6. Strain into the rocks glasses, filling half into each then topping off.
7. Garnish the glasses with lime wheel.

* Don't have a shaker set? Roll the cocktail with half the ice between two pint glasses four times, and then strain into the correct glassware, garnish and serve.

Make it your own! Notes...

Alternatives

Swap the grapefruit juice for pineapple juice.

Personal Tweaks

I should drink this with...

FLAMING RIVER

First Place Extinguish Cocktail Competition 2019

This was my third cocktail competition and a nerve-wracking day. The goal was to celebrate the health of the Cuyahoga River 50 years after the great fire. The rules were simple; incorporate the use of fire and the concept of fire into your cocktail. So I choose the vibrant color of pomegranate to pair with the warm spice of the Pope's Orange Habanero Cocktail Syrup. This is the same syrup that moved me out of the qualifying round to the finals. For the fire I used flash paper rolled into a river and mimicked the fire of 1969.

You Will Need:
1.5 oz Pope's Orange Habanero Cocktail Syrup
4 oz Cantera Negra Reposado Tequila
4 oz pomegranate juice
2 oz fresh lime juice
2 cups of ice, divided

Tools & Glassware:
2 rocks glasses
Hawthorne strainer
Shaker set*
Jigger

Garnish:
Half lime wheel
Pomegranate seeds

Method:
1. Measure liquids into the shaker.
2. Add half the ice to the shaker*.
3. Distribute the remaining ice evenly among two rocks glasses.
4. Shake until a light frost forms on the tin – roughly a 10 to 15 count.
5. Strain into your rocks glasses, filling half into each then topping off.
6. Garnish the glasses with lime wheel and a sprinkle of pomegranate seeds.

* Don't have a shaker set? Roll the cocktail with half the ice between two pint glasses four times, then strain into the correct glassware, garnish and serve.

Make it your own! Notes...

Alternatives
Swap the tequila for spiced rum

Personal Tweaks

I should drink this with...

BEER + BLOODY = A GOOD TIME

So many wonderful beer drinkers suffer each morning, watching their friends enjoy the brisk freshness of a Pope's bloody mary, sadly knowing that to order beers at 9:00 a.m. is just not socially acceptable. Fear not good people, for our friends south of the border bring you the Michelada, part Mexican lager, part bloody mary, 100% the socially acceptable way to start your day with a beer.

You Will Need:

6 oz. Pope's Bloody Mary Mix Bold & Spicy
24 oz beer / suggest an Mexican lager

Tools & Glassware:

2 pint glasses
Jigger
Bar spoon

Garnish:

Lime wheel
Optional rim of
 spiced salt

Method:

1. Rim Glass with spiced salt (optional)
2. Pour beer into pint glass
3. Top with Pope's Bloody Mary
4. Three stirs to combine with a spoon
5. Garnish with olives and shrimp skewer

Make it your own! Notes...

Alternatives

Swap a citrusy IPA for the Llager

Personal Tweaks

I should drink this with...

DRAGON'S TONGUE

The Dragon's Tongue was created to celebrate Cleveland Nights in Asia Town. It made its public debut at Night Market in summer of 2016 and became an instant classic. Watershed Bourbon Barrel Gin is the perfect pairing for the Orange-Habanero Syrup, as the citrus-forward gin, made with a botanical blend containing orange peel, lemon, lime, and grapefruit, rests in a bourbon barrel for one year, which brings out warm baking spice notes in addition to the herbal notes. The citrus and spice of the gin blends with the heat and sweetness of the syrup, resulting in a complex and surprisingly easy-drinking cocktail.

You Will Need:
1.5 oz Pope's Orange Habanero Syrup
3 oz Watershed Bourbon Barrel Gin
4 oz club soda
Ice

Tools & Glassware:
2 Collins glasses
Bar spoon
Jigger

Garnish:
Orange peel

Method:
1. Build drink directly in the glass.
2. Add ice to your collins glass.
3. Add Pope's Orange Habanero Cocktail Syrup, Gin, and top with club soda.
4. Stir from the bottom to combine thoroughly.
5. Garnish with orange peel.

Make it your own! Notes...

Alternatives
Want it spicier? Try adding a pinch of cayenne powder!

Personal Tweaks

I should drink this with...

LAVENDER PISCO SOUR

Peru is a wonderful country full of intense flavors and rife with a rich history, and the Pisco Sour is the national drink. Pisco is a Brandy that is the result of the Spanish planting grapevines in the 1500s and then some of the wine was distilled. It is believed to be named for the Port city of Pisco where it was shipped back to Spain. The original Pisco Sour was created by an American bartender in Lima, in the fall of 1916.

You Will Need:

2 oz Pope's Lavender Lemon Cocktail Syrup
5 oz Pisco
1 oz fresh lemon juice
2 egg whites
2 cups of ice, divided

Tools & Glassware:

2 Collins glasses
Hawthorne strainer
Shaker set
Jigger

Garnish:

Half a lime wheel
Dash of bitters on the foam

Method:

1. Add half the ice to the shaker.*
2. Pour Pope's Lavender Lemon Cocktail Syrup, Pisco, and lemon juice into the shaker.
3. Add egg whites to the shaker.
4. Distribute the remaining ice evenly among two Collins glasses.
5. Shake until a light frost forms on the tin – roughly a 10 to 15 count.
6. Strain beverage into the glasses, filling half into each then topping off.
7. Garnish the glasses with lime wheel.

* Don't have a shaker set? Roll the cocktail with half the ice between two pint glasses four times, and then strain into the correct glassware, garnish and serve.

Make it your own! Notes...

Alternatives

Instead of Pisco, use an Italian grappa. Brighten with lime juice in place of lemon juice.

Personal Tweaks

I should drink this with...

SOUTHERN FALL HARVEST

Kentucky is a state full of tradition, most of which involve friends and Bourbon. A long-standing tradition of celebrating hard work on warm summer nights is with smooth Bourbon drizzled over sweet ice cream. This allows the adults and children to both enjoy their ice cream. This unique flavor profile lives on in the bottles of Boone County Distillery Company's Bourbon Cream. Light the fire pits, fix up the s'mores, and enjoy this adult fall classic with friends.

You Will Need:
1.5 oz Pope's Pumpkin Spice Cocktail Syrup
3 oz Boone County Bourbon Cream
4 oz apple cider
2 cups of ice, divided

Tools & Glassware:
2 rocks glasses
Shaker set
Jigger

Garnish:
Thin apple slice

Method:
1. Divide half the ice among each glass.
2. Add remaining ice to the shaker*.
3. Pour Pope's Pumpkin Spice Cocktail Syrup, apple cider, and Bourbon Cream into the shaker.
4. Shake until a light frost forms on the tin – roughly a 10 to 15 count.
5. Strain beverage into rocks glasses.
6. Garnish the glasses with an apple slice.

*Don't have a shaker set? Roll the cocktail with half the ice between two pint glasses four times, then strain, garnish and serve.

Make it your own! Notes...

Alternatives
Add 1 oz of coffee liqueur.

Personal Tweaks

I should drink this with...

THE FRENCH RESISTANCE

As a former history teacher, I have always been intrigued by the hard work and valor of the brave French men and women who fought the Nazis after the fall of Paris. To celebrate these intrepid saboteurs, I reflected on my last trip to France, wanting to bring together all that I think of as French – the beautiful fields of Lavender, the fine bubbles of Champagne, and the rich warmth of Cognac. I give you a toast to those who resist.

You Will Need:

1 oz Pope's Lavender Lemon Cocktail Syrup
8 oz Champagne
2 oz cognac
1 cup of ice

Tools & Glassware:

2 Champagne flutes
Hawthorne strainer
Shaker set
Jigger

Garnish:

Half a lemon wheel

Method:

1. Measure Pope's Lavender Lemon Cocktail Syrup and cognac into the shaker.
2. Add 4 ice cubes to the shaker*.
3. Distribute the remaining ice evenly among two Champagne flutes.
4. Shake until a light frost forms on the tin – roughly a 10 to 15 count.
5. Discard ice from the glassware.
6. Strain beverage into Champagne flutes.
7. Top off each glass with Champagne. Pour slowly as it will bubble.
8. Garnish the glasses with lemon.

* Don't have a shaker set? Roll the cocktail with half the ice between two pint glasses four times, and then strain into the correct glassware, garnish and serve.

Make it your own! Notes...

Alternatives

Swap out Champagne for Sprite.
Swap out the cognac for gin.

Personal Tweaks

I should drink this with...

BLOODY GRILLED SHRIMP SHOOTER

There is something wonderful about how a hot wood fire can flavor shrimp. If you like a traditional shrimp cocktail, you will love a Bloody Grilled Shrimp Shooter. Serves 2.

You Will Need:
1 Cup Pope's Bloody Mary Mix Bold & Spicy, divided
10 large shrimps; peeled, deveined, with tails on
2 oz. vodka

Tools & Glassware:
2 grillable skewers
1 zip top bag
Tongs
2 small rocks glasses

Garnish:
Lemon wedge

Method:
1. Place clean, peeled shrimp with the tail on into a zip top bag.
2. Add half of the Bloody Mary Mix and let shrimp marinate for 30-45 minutes while your grill heats up.
3. Remove shrimp from bag and discard the marinade.
4. Thread the shrimp onto the skewers.
5. Grill the shrimp for 2 minutes on each side.
6. Remove from heat and let rest.
7. While the shrimp rests, divide the Vodka between the two rocks glasses, and pour the remaining Bloody Mary mix on top of the vodka.
8. Place five shrimp head down, tail out around each glass, and serve.

Make it your own! Notes...

Alternatives
Pre-prep for a party: chill the shrimp and serve the next day.
If you don't want it too spicy, use Pope's Traditional Bloody Mary Mix.

Personal Tweaks

I should share this with...

BLOODY MARY CHILI

The changing of leaves in the fall always brings me to my crockpot, creating simple meals that take little effort to prepare. Using the Pope's Bloody Mary Mix as a base removes 80% of the chili preparation, leaving that much more time for friends and family. Serves 6-8.

You Will Need:

1 Bottle Pope's Bloody Mary Mix Bold & Spicy
2 lbs. ground beef
1 large green pepper
1 large Spanish onion
1.5 tablespoons cumin
1 tablespoon salt
1 bay leaf
1 15 oz can light kidney beans
1 15 oz can dark kidney beans

Tools & Glassware:

Cutting board
Sharp knife
2 qt. slow cooker
Large spoon

Garnish:

Shredded cheese
Minced onion

Method:

1. Plug in and turn on the slow cooker to high.
2. Chop the onion and green pepper into ¼ inch pieces, put into slow cooker.
3. Add cumin and salt to the vegetables and stir.
4. Add the ground beef, and use your spoon to break it up.
5. Drain and rinse the beans, add to the slow cooker, and stir.
6. Pour 1 bottle of Pope's Bloody Mary Mix over everything and stir.
7. Add bay leaf.
8. Cover with lid and turn cock pot to medium heat if possible and cook for 6 – 8 hours.
9. After 6-8 hours, remove lid, turn off slow cooker and stir, allowing mixture to absorb any liquids.
10. Serve warm or pack into containers and put in the fridge for up to one week.

Make it your own! Notes...

Alternatives

Use black beans or chickpeas
Use Pope's Traditional instead of Bold & Spicy

Personal Tweaks

I should share this with...

BLOODY SHRIMP DIABLO

Shrimp may be one of my most favorite foods. Bubba from Forest Gump, said it best when he recited twenty-three different uses for shrimp, but he forgot the best and easiest. Sauté it quickly with Pope's Bloody Mary Bold and Spicy Mix, toss in some handmade pasta, and you have great meal in less than ten minutes. Serves 2.

You Will Need:

1 cup Pope's Bloody Mary Mix Bold & Spicy
4-8 oz fresh pasta
18 large shrimps; peeled, deveined, tails removed
1 tablespoon oil

Tools & Glassware:

Measuring cup
Pasta pot
Tongs
9 inch sauté pan

Garnish:

Chopped parsley
Lemon wedge

Method:

1. Follow directions for your pasta. Fresh pasta should cook for roughly 3 – 4 minutes.
2. When the water comes to a boil add the pasta.
3. Heat your sauté pan.
4. Add oil, when oil shimmers, add shrimp, and cook one side 2 minutes.
5. Turn the shrimp and cook 1 minute.
6. Add Pope's Bloody Mary Mix and cook 1 minute.
7. Turn off heat, pull the pasta from the pot with your tongs shake off excess water, and stir pasta into the shrimp and sauce.
8. Garnish with chopped parsley and lemon wedge. Serve.

Make it your own! Notes...

Alternatives

Use scallops with or in place of shrimp
Meat-free with Pope's Bloody Vegan Mix and tofu

Personal Tweaks

I should share this with...

BUTTER

For those of you who have not met me, you may be surprised to learn that the guy who makes his living by cooking and making cocktails is a bit heavy set. Many well-meaning people often lecture me on using alternatives to real food in my diet. But you know what they say about good intentions, so I respond to their unsolicited advice with a rebuttal on margarine and why it should not be consumed by humans. As the founder of Pope's Kitchen, I am proud that I only use real food in my products – and, yes, life needs a balance between consumption and exercise. That aside, let's look at the simplicity of real food. Take butter for instance; it is a simple trick of whipping liquid cream into a solid. Just one ingredient plus energy gives you the real thing that has so much flavor and texture! Margarine, on the other hand, needs a laboratory, nine ingredients, and a marketing campaign to convince you that it "tastes like the real thing."

You Will Need:
8 oz Heavy Whipping Cream
1.5 oz Pope's Lavender Lemon Cocktail Syrup
.5 teaspoon fresh thyme, leaves stripped

Tools & Glassware:
Mixing bowl
Whisk or electric beaters
Cheesecloth

Use Or:
Fresh bread, roasted meats, steamed vegetables

Method:
1. The key to easy butter to is ensure everything is cold, so place your cream, whisk/beaters, the bowl, and cocktail syrup into the fridge for at least 10 minutes before you start the whole process.
2. When everything is adequately chilled, pour cream into the bowl.
3. Add cocktail syrup to the cream.
4. Whisk/beat briskly. In about 3 minutes it will become whipped cream, keep whisking/beating until it breaks at about 5 minutes, you will have butter solids and buttermilk. Pour off about 4 oz of the liquid, or save for another use.
5. Add thyme leaves, whisk/beat for one more minute to incorporate and distribute throughout.
6. Pour off any remaining liquid, and wrap the solids in cheesecloth.
7. Squeeze until no more liquid comes out.
8. Store butter in an air tight container in the refrigerator, butter will keep for several days.

Make it your own! Notes...

Alternatives
Substitute any other Pope's Cocktail Syrup, or fresh thyme.

Personal Tweaks

I should share this with...

DIRTY MEDITERRANEAN SALAD

In the summer, I love the fresh flavors of the garden. No tomatoes are as sweet, nor the cucumbers as crisp as when they are freshly picked. It was not until after college that I learned about how delicious feta could be (Thank you, Tom Nahra!). Blending these favorites together makes for a wonderfully fresh salad or side dish. Here is a quick and easy way to bring a little summer to your table.

You Will Need:

3 oz Pope's Dirty Martini Blend
8 oz chickpeas
2 large cucumbers
Half of a large red onion
3 large tomatoes
Half a bunch of Italian parsley
8 oz by weight, feta cheese
8 oz by weight, pitted olives

Tools & Glassware:

Gallon zip top Bag
Serving bowl
Cutting board
Sharp knife

Garnish:

Lemon wedges

Method:

1. Chop cucumbers and tomatoes into ¼ inch pieces and place into a zip top bag.
2. Dice red onion into 1/4 inch pieces and add to bag.
3. Slice olives into thirds and to bag.
4. Drain chickpeas and add to bag.
5. Add Pope's Dirty Martini Blend to the bag. Seal, and lay the bag flat to increase contact with the vegetables.
6. Allow vegetables to marinate at least 30 minutes on the counter, flipping over occasionally.
7. While the vegetables get friendly in the bag, slice the feta into ¼ inch pieces and roughly chop the parsley.
8. When ready, pour mixture from bag into a serving bowl, stir in the feta and parsley.
9. Garnish with lemons and serve.

Make it your own! Notes...

Alternatives

Leave out the chickpeas.
Add a splash of dry vermouth.

Personal Tweaks

I should eat this with...

POPE'S PAELLA

Paella is a traditional dish of Valencia Spain often made with fresh seafood, rice, and tomatoes in large batches using special pans over wood fires. Not having a large number of special pans for specific dishes, I have made a few changes to this traditional dish-my apologies to the people of Spain. Serves 6-8.

You Will Need:

1 Bottle Pope's Bloody Mary Mix Bold & Spicy
24 oz chicken broth
6 oz white wine
2 lbs. chicken breasts
1 lb. large shrimps; peeled, deveined, tails removed
2 dozen fresh mussels
6 oz chorizo
1 large green pepper
1 large Spanish onion
4 garlic cloves
3 cups rice
2 tablespoon of olive oil (divided)
2 oz lemon juice

Tools & Glassware:

Cutting board
Sharp knife
8-qt pot
4-qt pot
Plates for resting items
Tea towel

Garnish:

Lemon wedges
Fresh minced parsley
Fresh baguette

Method:

1. Mix together the chicken broth and Pope's Bloody Mary Mix in the 4-qt pot, and bring to a simmer.
2. While this simmers, finely dice the pepper, onion, and garlic. Slice the Chorizo and chicken and set aside.
3. In the 8-qt pot, add 1 tablespoon of olive oil and heat to a shimmer.
4. Add the chicken and cook for four minutes, remove, and set aside.
5. Add the chorizo and cook for two minutes, remove, and set aside.
6. Add the shrimp and cook for two minutes, remove, and set aside.
7. Add remaining olive oil to the 8-qt pot, and add the diced vegetables. Sauté until softened, about 10 minutes.
8. Add in the liquid from the 4-qt pot and bring to a simmer.
9. Add the rice and bring to a low boil for 10 minutes, stirring occasionally.
10. Add the mussels, stirring them into the rice, and cook for 5 minutes.
11. Remove any mussels that have not opened, add back in the chicken, chorizo, and shrimp, stirring into the rice, and cook for 5 minutes.
12. Drizzle with the lemon juice. Remove from heat, and cover with a tea towel for 10 minutes.

SODAS

Personally, I find that one of the best things about creating all-natural cocktail syrups from real food is that they make great sodas. They're refreshing and simple, and they don't contain chemical additives, colors, or flavors.

You Will Need:

2 oz Pope's Cocktail Syrup – Any Flavor
10 oz club soda
2 cups of ice, divided

Tools & Glassware:

2 Collins glasses
Bar spoon
Jigger

Garnish:

Half lemon, lime, or orange Wheel

Method:

1. Distribute the ice evenly among the glasses.
2. Add 1 oz of Pope's Cocktail Syrup to each glass.
3. Pour 5 oz club soda over ice and syrup.
4. Use the bar spoon to gently stir to blend.
5. Garnish the glasses with fruit wheel.

SPANISH CHICKEN

I love chicken, but it has gotten a bad reputation from overuse and abuse. For some reason, "everything" tastes like chicken. Not this chicken! I import the olive brine from Spain for Pope's Dirty Martini Blend, so I created a chicken dish celebrating Spain and featuring that lovely olive flavor.

You Will Need:

4 oz Pope's Dirty Martini Blend
1.5 oz olive oil
8 chicken thighs, skin on
8 cloves fresh garlic, divided
Half of a Spanish onion
9 sprigs of fresh rosemary
6 oz dry white wine
8 oz by weight, pitted Spanish olives
1 teaspoon freshly ground black pepper
2 oz lemon juice
1 cup of rice

Tools & Glassware:

Oven-safe pan with lid
Plate for seared chicken
Cutting board
Sharp knife
Whisk or wooden spoon
Tongs
Serving platter

Garnish:

Lemon wedges
Fresh rosemary sprigs

Method:

1. Pre-heat oven to 400.
2. Thinly slice the Spanish onion, mince 4 cloves of garlic, and set aside.
3. Lightly season the chicken thighs lightly with ground pepper and set aside.
4. Add olive oil to the pan over medium-high heat.
5. When oil shimmers, add the chicken thighs skin side down. Sear for 8 minutes, and then turn for 2 more minutes.
6. Remove chicken and set aside.
7. Add minced garlic and sliced onion to the pan and sauté in the remaining fat for about 2 minutes.
8. Deglaze by adding Pope's Dirty Martini Blend, white wine, and lemon juice to the pan.
9. Add to the pan the rice, the remaining 4 whole cloves of garlic, and the olives.
10. Add the chicken and any juice on the plate to the pan.
11. Add rosemary sprigs on to the top of the chicken thighs, cover with a lid, and simmer for 5 minutes.
12. Place in the oven for 20 minutes.
13. After baking, pull the pan from the oven and check chicken for doneness.
14. Remove the chicken and rest for 3 minutes.
15. Plate by laying the chicken over the rice and olives and garnish with fresh lemon wedges and rosemary.

STEAK IT DIRTY

Growing up in the 80's, I learned a few things from watching TV—milk does a body good and beef is what's for dinner. It was not a good decade to be a cow, was it? There are lots of ways to have beef for dinner, and here is a steak preparation, which can then be used for many dishes. Since I love the saltiness of olives and the rich texture of a medium-rare steak. What better way to achieve this than to marinate a steak in Pope's Dirty Martini Blend, seasoned with fresh pepper and herbs? I like to serve this with roasted baby red potatoes.

You Will Need:
3 oz Pope's Dirty Martini Blend
2 6-8 oz steaks
1 teaspoon freshly ground black pepper
1 teaspoon dried oregano

Tools & Glassware:
1 zip top Bag
Sauté pan or grill
Tongs

Garnish:
Fresh parsley, chopped
Lemon wedge

Method:
1. Place the steaks into the zip top bag and cover them with Pope's Dirty Martini Blend.
2. Set aside for 30 minutes at room temperature while you prepare your side dish.
3. Remove steaks from the bag and season with freshly ground pepper and oregano on each side.
4. Preheat the pan over medium-high heat.
5. Add a tablespoon of oil to the pan and sear the steaks for about 3 minutes per side.
6. Remove steaks from the pan, and let them rest for 3 minutes while plating the side dishes.
7. Serve with fresh parsley and a lemon wedge.

Make it your own! Notes...

Alternatives
Thinly slice the steak and use for a sandwich or fajitas.

Personal Tweaks

I should share this with...

WHIPPED CREAM

I am not sure what it is that makes cream such a special item in my life, but if I had to say one thing it is the simplicity of it. Cream is the top layer that is skimmed from fresh cow's milk and contains roughly 35% fat—vastly different from the 2% milk I grew up drinking. This simple difference allows us to create whipped cream, butter, and ice cream just by adding in a few simple steps. Beat heavy cream with a whisk and it will double in volume and create soft peaks to capture fresh berries in at breakfast. Beat a little longer, and you get stiff peaks perfect for angel food cake and more berries. Add a little sugar and flavoring, you have a whole new experience.

You Will Need:
8 oz heavy whipping cream
1.5 oz Pope's Blueberry Lemon Cocktail Syrup

Tools & Glassware:
Mixing bowl

Garnish:
Fresh berries
Whisk or electric beaters

Method:
1. The key to easy whipped cream to is ensure everything is cold, so place your cream, whisk/beaters, the bowl, and cocktail syrup into the fridge for at least 10 minutes before you start the whole process.
2. When everything is adequately chilled, pour cream into the bowl.
3. Add cocktail syrup to the cream.
4. Whisk/beat briskly until peaks form to desired stiffness. On high speed this takes me about three minutes.
5. Gently transfer the whipped cream to a serving bowl or place back into the fridge until time for dessert.
6. Whipped cream will keep for 2 days covered in the fridge.

Make it your own! Notes...

Alternatives
Substitute any of the Pope's Cocktail Syrups for the Blueberry Lemon Syrup

Personal Tweaks

I should share this with...

SOURCES AND ACKNOWLEDGEMENTS

Pope's cocktail products are available in stores throughout Ohio, and online.

Our home store is Merchants Mrkt in Legacy Village

Online, we can be found at:
www.popeskitchen.com
princeofscots.com and
Amazon.com, listed in the grocery & gourmet food category

Acknowledgments

I must say that a book is not created on its own. Thank you to the many people that have made this project a reality. Allison, who pushed for a book to support her sales of my products at her store Cleveland in a Box. Shannon Okey, my dear friend, thank you for supporting my business and all of the designers and makers of both the wonderful Cleveland Bazaar and Cooperative Press. Your encouragement has made it possible for a decade of creators to share and express ourselves through the printed word. Thank you for publishing this book, I would not have done this with anyone else. Matt Bailey, I so want to add a few extra commas, here, thank you for your editing and re-editing of my babbling. The lovely pictures come from the talent of Jeremy Fear, it was a great weekly adventure, I promise to never change the prefix of a file again, thank you.

This adventure has also taken the strength and time of many dear friends.

Thank you to Matt Montecalvo for your daily interventions, Chris Ilcin for your marketing and social media interventions, Mike Washlock for your literal strength and creativity, Steph Washlock for your unwavering support of all my ideas, both amazing and not so much. It should always be said loudly and often, thank you to my dear wife, Sarah, who shoulders all of my delusions of greatness and allows me to chase this dream. Thank you to my mom Joyce for all of her support and encouragement, and thank you to my sister Jennifer for always having my back. To my dearest Meredith, you will always be my favorite bear, thank you.

www.ingramcontent.com/pod-product-compliance
Lightning Source LLC
Chambersburg PA
CBHW060948170426
43201CB00024B/2422